Black Boy Fly

by

Malcolm E. Daniels

Looking back, all I can say is thank you father God for bringing me out of the jungle that I've seen many of my friends get lost and eaten in. – Malcolm E. Daniels

Introduction

This is the story of a young boy named Messiah Dennis who had a pretty stable upbringing, but unfortunately, like so many black and brown boys, Messiah got lost in the dangerous but enticing excitement of the streets. Messiah was vulnerable and easily influenced which eventually took his life on an interesting ride until he finally woke up from the hypnotized fantasy that the streets had him under.

Chapter 1

Born on August 25, 1994, Messiah was born to Krystle and Marcus Dennis. Marcus and Krystle already birthed two other children: Kristie and little Marcus, making Messiah the youngest of three. Growing up in the suburbs of Washington DC, Messiah had a really exciting and adventurous upbringing. Messiah was into playing sports, hanging around the neighborhood with his siblings and friends, but he enjoyed family vacations the most and he was blessed to go on plenty of them. Messiah went to Disney World, New York, and Atlanta as a kid. Messiah was not a spoiled brat type of kid; he enjoyed the simple things like skating in the garage with his big sister Kristie while Grandpa Gary played oldies but goodies. Messiah's parents, Big Marcus and Krystle, where considered upper middle class citizens; they were not rich, but they certainly created a comfortable lifestyle for their kids. From the outside looking in, the Dennis family seemed to be the picture-perfect family. From the time Messiah was born until about the age of eight years old, he lived like a king in a castle, Messiah felt he had the perfect life and didn't want anything to change. Messiah's life was almost perfect; he never went to sleep hungry, every Christmas he got new presents, and he had all of the new bike's and gadgets on the block before all of the other kids. However, change was on the way to the family's picture-perfect lifestyle.

Chapter 2

Big Marcus and Krystle got a divorce and this crushed Messiah, Kristie, and little Marcus. It came so sudden they didn't even see the signs right before their eyes. Messiah and his older sister Kristie moved with Krystle to another suburb in Maryland. Messiah's older brother little Marcus stayed with big Marcus in the family's home for a little while until they eventually went to live with Messiah's grandmother, big Marcus's mother. Eventually Messiah found out that Krystle was seeing another man named Tommy and that's what led to the divorce along with other things that Messiah was too young to understand. Messiah had never heard of Tommy before the divorce, of course his parents weren't letting the kids in on grown folks' business. This is the event that started to spark a rage in young Messiah that he never knew was there. All three of the kids where affected the most by the split and, it really tainted Kristie's and Messiah's relationship with little Marcus. Messiah especially wanted to live with his big brother, he couldn't imagine life without little Marcus every day and later on in Messiah's story, he will find himself really needing the guidance from little Marcus. After things where handled in court, Krystle and big Marcus agreed that Kristie and Messiah would visit big Marcus every other weekend. Shortly after things calmed down, Krystle married Tommy.

Young Messiah was devastated; he didn't fully understand the circumstances of divorces and breakups, but he did understand that his mother was dating another man who was not big Marcus and he didn't appreciate that. Messiah treated things like they hadn't changed; he thought that Big Marcus was still the only man that could tell him what to do and he stayed loyal to his father. Tommy was completely different from Big Marcus. He had feminist ways if you asked Messiah. Tommy was the type of guy who wanted all of the attention from Krystle and didn't want to leave any for the kids. Tommy was not family oriented, at least to the kids, maybe because Messiah and Kristie were not his own, but whatever it was, he didn't receive any respect from Kristie and Messiah because of it.

Chapter 3

In the new neighborhood, Messiah eventually met a number of friends but his best friends where Raesse and Shine. They all came from somewhat of a similar background. Raesse was an only child in his home; he did have a older brother but he didn't live with him, which was ironically the situation that Messiah has become a part of. Raesse lived with his single mother because, his father was killed. Shine had two brothers but he only lived with the younger one and his mother; his father was locked up. Messiah and Shine where the same age and, Raesse was a year older than them. All these young black boys were missing their older brothers and that will probably be a issue later on. They all seemed to think they were the man of their homes, despite whoever their mothers where dating. They all were in elementary school when they met and they were into sports trying to find their way as young men without their biological fathers in the house. Messiah was the only one who had a solid relationship with his father, as a matter of fact, Big Marcus was more involved with Messiah than Tommy could ever be and he lived miles away. Big Marcus made many sacrifices to stay in Messiah's life constantly. He drove from an hour's distance to get Messiah to football practice three times out the week and was at every Saturday game. Tommy never attended any of Messiah's games and it didn't bother Messiah as long as Big Marcus was present. As the trio entered middle school, they started to be attracted to pretty girls and they were ready for the preteen and teenage life ahead. They started with the innocent activities like house parties, hanging at the skating rink, and hanging with friends at the mall and movies. At first, it was all so innocent and fun. Their mothers stayed in contact to make sure that the boys weren't running game and they were safe. This worked for a little while.

Chapter 4

Even though Big Marcus was just a couple of miles up the road and a phone call away, he couldn't protect young Messiah from what the world was about to offer. Messiah just being in the presence of his father a couple of times monthly was not enough to keep him out of trouble. As the trio entered high school still by each other's side, they all started to find their own way. They were all interested in the same things, but their personalities were all different. Shine was the aggressive one; he was a leader. Whatever he wanted to pursue, he would go after it. Shine was the only one who joined the high school football team, which was ironic because they all loved football and played for the Pop Warner league. Raesse was into being cool with the girls and fashion. Raesse was not really interested in school at all and it started to show. Messiah was the lost soul; he was the brightest academically, but he didn't have the mindset that Shine had to be a leader. Messiah actually wanted to join the football team with Shine but he was too busy chasing Raesse. One day, one of Messiah's teachers approached him about joining the wrestling team; he explained that Messiah had the perfect shape and frame for the sport and he also had the grades. Messiah was too ashamed to go on the wrestling team. He knew that wouldn't be cool in the eyes of his friends, so he denied the offer. After the football season was over, Shine seemed to lose focus on school along with Raesse. One day, little Marcus, who was probably twenty one at the time, came to take the boys to school. As they pulled up to the school, Raesse and Shine got out and headed for Shine's house.

Messiah had this look on his face as if he wanted to join, his older brother little Marcus killed that thought instantly. This is the guidance that Messiah needed every day, without Big Marcus and little Marcus, Messiah was adopting bad habits. Messiah saw Raesse later on in the school day in the hallway outside of the principal's office; he knew something went wrong. Raesse explain to Messiah that they got caught skipping school walking from Shine's house to Raesse's house. Messiah's grades where really good, despite his friends not having the work ethic that he had for school, so he seemed to be able to stay cool with his friends and stay on top of his work. Many people were not sure how Messiah's grades were so good and Raesse's grades where struggling; in fact, Raesse's mother urged Messiah to help Raesse with his school work. Messiah tried to follow her instructions, but Raesse was not interested in school and Messiah couldn't make him do his work. So Raesse's grades continued to suffer. Eventually, Shine and Raesse ended up failing their freshman year of high school and had to attend summer school. This was only the beginning of the downward spiral in Raesse and Shine's lives.

Chapter 5

Going into Messiah's sophomore year in high school he finally moved in with Big Marcus. Big Marcus was newly married to Messiah's stepmother Robin. Messiah was excited about the move, unlike his abandoned relationship with his stepfather Tommy, Messiah actually liked Robin. After Messiah, Shine, and Raesse ran wild the whole summer, Krystle recognized that Messiah was growing out of control and needed to be with his father and older brother. Around this time social media was becoming popular on the scene, in which the trio was very active on. Raesse and Messiah, one day, came across Raesse's older cousin Carlton on Myspace. The two couldn't help but admire Carlton. Carlton was only a year older than Raesse and two years older than Messiah, but his lifestyle seemed so out of reach to the two of them. Carlton was a drug dealer in a public housing neighborhood in Southeast DC.

Raesse reached out to Carlton and they chatted. Eventually

Carlton invited Raesse and Messiah to the neighborhood with

open arms. This was the beginning of some of the most

reckless years of Messiah's life. Even though he was now

living in the house with his dad and big brother, he was

interested in what the streets had to offer. Messiah had

already committed to being a follower in his past years without

Big Marcus and little Marcus in his presence every day.

Shortly after Carlton had the conversation with Raesse,

Raesse and Messiah took a visit to the neighborhood.

Messiah had never seen anything like it up close and

personal. Walking through the hood, Messiah was shook a

little after being confronted by the block boys. As Messiah and

Raesse walked through the hallways in the buildings, there

where groups of guys just staring at them as if they were

intruders. Carlton made it clear that these where his little

cousins so they were unharmed in the jungle. Messiah, the

once great student and baby boy of the family, was now

exposed to the fast street life. The thing that was so

interesting about the hood kids that Messiah and Raesse

shortly created relationships with was how different their lifestyle's where from the two of them even though, they were around the same age. The neighborhood kids where already smoking, rolling dice, and selling drugs. Raesse and Messiah got exposed to different avenues from the neighborhood every time they went around the way.

Chapter 6

Messiah was introduced to drugs, sex, and alcohol, all by the tender age of 15. Messiah was almost locked up several times. One day, Messiah and Raesse was in the Macys at the mall. Messiah had his eyes on this shirt and he had the money to buy it, but he thought it would be a smoother transaction if he stole it, while Raesse just laughed as they headed for the door, Messiah was approached by two men who he eventually found out were undercover officers for the store. That was Messiah's first real trouble, besides suspensions in middle school. Messiah could've never seen his self in handcuffs before this day. Messiah was held at the store until Krystle came and picked him up and he could tell she was mad as hell. Right then Messiah knew he was giving Krystle real trouble. Krystle and Messiah had a solid mother and son relationship; their loyalty to each other was spectacular; therefore, an incident like the one Messiah had just experienced stayed between the two and didn't reach Big Marcus until sometime later. All three of the friends were on a downhill spiral and after sometime, their parents started to get hip. Krystle, Raesse's mother, and Shine's mother would sometimes ask to talk to each other to confirm where the boys where going and who was taking and picking them up from their destination. The three found ways to slip through the cracks of being trapped in the suburbs and having limits put on what they had access to. The boys came up with a plan to find ways to stay in the projects as long as they wanted. Messiah's grandfather, Gary, Krystle's father, lived just across the bridge in southeast from the projects where they now called home. This was the perfect plot for the boys! They knew they would never be allowed to hang in the projects, but they were allowed to stay at Grandpa Gary's for the weekend.

Messiah, Raesse, and Shine were suburban kids during the weekdays when they went to school and block boys by Friday night. Their lifestyles were similar to NuNu from the hit movie *ATL. It was all a front. Like NuNu's father in ATL, their parents all grew up in the city,* so they thought that meant they had the privilege of bragging about experiences that they never faced. The thing that the trio didn't understand is that times had changed from the era their parents grew up in and, things were a lot more reckless and dangerous in today's time. The boy's seemed blinded to the fact that there was danger lurking all around their surroundings. The funny thing about it is that they would laugh at other adolescents who they went to school with who claimed they were from the city like they were jokes. The people who grew up in the city were always seen as cooler than the suburban kids. Most of the suburban kids that Messiah, Raesse, and Shine went to school with only seen the lifestyle of the city kids from social media. Messiah, Shine, and Raesse actually transformed into city kids. They learned the dos and don'ts and started living by the street code.

Chapter 7

Shine, always the fast and ambitious one, started selling marijuana which led him to another part of the city where he started to frequently hang. Messiah and Raesse would venture out to Shine's new hangout from time to time, but it just wasn't as comfortable as the projects where Carlton and the rest of the neighborhood crew was that they had grown to love. Another new factor had come into Shine's life; he reunited with his big brother Dee who was locked up in previous years. Shine's ways started to change. He started to see what his brother and older cousins where doing and shortly after that, he got involved. Dee was the complete opposite of little Marcus; he pulled his little brother into the lifestyle that little Marcus was protecting Messiah from. Shine started drinking heavy and would sometimes show up to the projects to meet Raesse and Messiah pissy drunk, this kind of made Messiah and Raesse embarrassed because the guys in the projects would harass Shine. One time, they almost stripped him naked that was the way the neighborhood guys would treat sloppy drunk people . Messiah was disappointed in Shine; he knew that they all were doing stuff they shouldn't have, but he could have never imagined one of his bestfriends falling into such a deep sorrow as he did. The thing about it is that Messiah was not a leader at the time; instead, Messiah was caught up in his own sins and was too weak minded to offer his friend a better way. It seemed that Raesse didn't really mind the change in Shine's behavior. Messiah, on the other hand, was becoming skeptical of even hanging with Shine. Messiah knew that serious trouble was on the brink. The biggest thing that made Messiah uncomfortable was Shine's brother and his older cousins. They seemed to stay off the liquor and they would get into altercations everywhere they went. See it was different in the projects; Messiah was comfortable there even though they were doing no better than Shine and his crew. Messiah and Raesse where a part of the neighborhood by now; they were no longer outcasts in the projects. At this stage in the trio's lives they were all living out their fantasies in real life. The gang was having the time of their lives, going to every Go-Go in the city, hanging with

Carlton and the hood boys, and having all of the girls. Every time the neighborhood went to the Go-Go they would all put their money together and get the VIP section, Messiah was having the time of his life. Everything that Messiah ever wanted or thought he wanted, he had. The three loved going back to school on Mondays bragging about what they had experienced over the weekend; this made the boys feel good about their selves as if they had accomplished something. At school, the boys were popular; they were even known as city kids. Everything was not always comfortable in the neighborhood though. Messiah once was in the middle of a gun transaction when one of his friends was selling Carlton a gun. After Carlton brought the gun, he put the gun to Messiah's head; he was only playing, but Messiah couldn't help but see his life flash before him. Messiah knew that it could have ended right then and there, but that only added to the excitement in his immature mind. Messiah loved the thrill; his whole life, he was only exposed to the suburban lifestyle for the most part. He was so happy that he was being accepted by the hood.

Chapter 8

Messiah was fortunate enough to not get caught in the drug game, but he did use, just never sold. Messiah was all about the fun; he didn't want to be violent or a criminal, he just wanted to be in the action, wherever the party and the action was. Raesse was living his fantasy as well, being next to his cousin Carlton; he thought he was on top of the world. However little did the gang know, things were about to change. Yet again another major change in Messiah's life was on its way. Grandpa Gary started getting sick and he started putting limits on Messiah's freedom at his house. One night, Messiah was hanging in the projects, just chillin hard with the homies, he eventually made his way across the bridge to grandpa's house and grandpa was there waiting for him. He told Messiah if you want to continue to stay over, you now have a curfew. He told Messiah he needed to be in the house by 12:00am, which wasn't too bad for a 16 year old and at the time the curfew in DC for kids under 17 was 10:00pm.Still this was slowing Messiah up, Messiah felt things where changing because grandpa used to be the coolest man on Earth, he would let Messiah have a sip of the 40 if he wanted. Grandpa also grew irritated of Raesse staying at his house. He knew that Messiah was a follower and that running with Raesse was a clear example of the blind leading the blind. Grandpa Gary wanted Messiah to be a strong young man; he knew that Messiah had the potential. Grandpa Gary lost his son, Messiah's uncle Reynaldo years earlier he got kilt in the Army. Grandpa Gary somewhat looked at Messiah as his own son and it was a disappointment to him that Messiah was following behind someone who wasn't offering him intelligence and positivity. As grandpa got sicker to Messiah, he got meaner and a lot less tolerate. Grandpa even reached out to Big Marcus to express that he needed to watch Raesse around Messiah. A couple of weeks later, Grandpa Gary got diagnosed with throat cancer. This was a heavy blow to the whole family. Grandpa was very much the backbone of the family, and to Messiah, his house was access to his hood dreams. After a few visits to the Howard Hospital Center in Washington DC, Krystle got the call that Grandpa Gary passed away. Messiah was now in the 12th grade. He barely had contact with Shine and Raesse anymore. One thing that really bothered Messiah is how Raesse didn't bother to go with the family to visit Grandpa while he was sick in the hospital or even attend the funeral, but he was ready to spend the weekend at grandpa's house to run wild in the streets.

Chapter 9

The death of Grandpa Gary changed everything for Messiah, for a lack of a better expression, he became woke and started to see things and people for what they really were. Messiah finally started to become a leader and make his own path. Things started to turn around drastically for Messiah; he got his first part time job at Safeway; he got his provisional license; and he was on a mission to get a scholarship to attend college. After Krystle noticed the responsibility that Messiah was now taking on, she let him drive one of her vehicles, fresh after getting his license. As time passed, Messiah lost contact with his longtime friends Raesse and

Shine for good. Messiah would sometimes on a rare occasion, run into Raesse at his job at the Safeway. Raesse would ask "Wassup with you?" You don't fool with us anymore?" What Raesse failed to understand is that Messiah had grown apart from him, Shine and all of that negativity that he was once excited to be a part of. Messiah tried to get his point across in a respectful demeanor, but Raesse couldn't see things for what they really were. Messiah felt his words where going in one ear and out the other. Messiah did go around the neighborhood one more time after Grandpa's passing and he realized that it too had to be cut off. Messiah seemed happy to be around the projects for the last time; however, Messiah was happy that God had exposed him to the street life and Messiah was able to become aware that this life was not meant for him, Messiah believed that this life was not meant for anyone. Messiah eventually surrounded himself with people who he thought would benefit his next steps into becoming a strong young man. Messiah was now running with two brothers Jermain and Kain who were both younger than him, Jermain was one year younger than Messiah and

Kain was three years younger than Messiah. Messiah saw an opportunity in befriending the brothers to save them from falling into the hype of the street life as Messiah had previously done. Messiah wished he would have taken a better route and saved time and energy. Messiah did keep in touch with one of his friends from previous years, Rayvon. Rayvon used to hang with Messiah, Raesse, and Shine when they were all together, but Rayvon did actually live in the city, so he never had to fake it. Messiah looked up to Rayvon who was two years his senior. Rayvon went to school with Carlton and other guys from the projects and he knew them before Messiah even started hanging around them, so he was really close to the streets and knew what they were about. Rayvon seemed to see something special in Messiah. Rayvon did something that none of the guys in the neighborhood ever would have done, he encouraged Messiah to be himself and follow his dreams. He told Messiah that he was better than sitting on the corner all day. Messiah loved Rayvon for that and he started to put his plans in motion.

Chapter 10

Messiah was already a motivated young man, but once he got that extra push from an outside source other than Big Marcus and little Marcus, Messiah was ready to take control of his life. Messiah graduated from high school, kept working at Safeway, enrolled into a community college and brought his own car. While walking across the stage at graduation, all Messiah could think about was Grandpa Gary. He knew that he would have been in the crowd cheering and causing chaos because his youngest grandchild was going across the stage. Messiah kept pressing the envelope to expand and grow. By the age of 19, Messiah was now working for the United States Postal Service as a mailman. He really was creating a successful life for himself. Messiah would occasionally run into mutual friends from old relationships he had with Raesse and Shine and he would hear what their lives were like and just wonder *could he save them before it's too late.* Through all of the change that Messiah had experienced within a year, Raesse and Shine seemed to still be stuck on the same negative path that was now behind Messiah. Some of Messiah's new friends would see Raesse and Shine over social media still portraying the lifestyle as if they were raised in the same environment in which Carlton was. The ironic thing about this story is that both Raesse and Shine actually where raised in the same fashion as Carlton, maybe not from parents who held the same values, but they were all raised by females for the majority of their lives. The young black males typically turn to the streets for teachings in which they are not being taught in the households. Messiah had a father in the house for the majority of his life, but that little gap of time in which his father was not under the same roof as him led to him getting distracted. This is a critical lesson that Messiah wants to share with the world to inspire the real men of the world who have a positive voice or want to push positivity into young males to step up into some of these lost boys with no positive role models in their lives. Messiah once ran into a mutual friend who also had relations with Raesse and Shine; they started chatting. She said, "What's going on with you and your friends?" Messiah downplayed the situation because he truly didn't have an issue with Raesse nor Shine. She told Messiah that she ran into Shine a while back and asked him the same question, but his response was a lot different and hostile, he told her that he did not fuck with Messiah. Although there was negative energy coming from Raesse and Shine, Messiah was able to stay positive about the situation; he knew that he was doing the right thing and he moved on for the better, he just wished they would wake up and get on the same train before it passed them by. Messiah also learned that Raesse and Shine both had babies by the age of 19, neither of the two was married and they both still lived at home. *This is way too common in the black community Messiah* thought. No one is taught the value of real love anymore. We, as young black men, are taught to get all of the sex we can and never catch feelings. Messiah learned that Raesse and Shine turned out to be the same young black men that Big Marcus was trying to stir him away from. They ended up lost in the society that young black urban boys all too often get lost in.

Chapter 11

A couple of years later, Messiah got the phone call that he knew he would eventually get. Shine was murdered! This was heartbreaking to Messiah even though he had not talked to Shine in about 4 years, the love was still there if you asked Messiah. Messiah just started reminiscing about the innocent times they shared as young twelve-year-old boys playing football and running around in school, everything seemed so easy then. It seems like when you are young, you are exempt from serious crime and violence. Messiah could have never imagined losing one of his friends when he was twelve. It all started to come together for Messiah. The change he started to see in his friend Shine eventually took his young life. Shine was misguided for the most of his life; there was a blank space in his mind and, he lacked the education of what it meant to be a real man. This tragic event forced Messiah to turn spiritual; he knew that God could answer all his questions and conquer all of his fears. Messiah started to feel that he was put on this earth for a greater purpose. As years continued to come and go, he still received calls about guys from the projects that was once his stomping ground a couple of years ago getting locked up and murdered. Most of the guys that used to hang out in the projects with Messiah were incarcerated and, some had died. The sad reality is Messiah knew what was in store for most of them. One of the saddest calls that Messiah received, other than the call about Shine, was a call about Carlton. Yep, Messiah got the call that the almighty guy that he once worshiped and looked up to got killed outside of the housing projects that he lived in a ran for so many years. Jay Z has a line in his song *The Story of OJ* *that says "don't die over the neighborhood that your momma's* *renting."* This exact line is so important to the urban communities but most will overlook the jewel dropped by the talented rapper. Unfourtunaley many young black males all too often make this mistake that Jay Z is telling us not to do. Shine was 21 years old when he got killed, Carlton was 24. This was so heinous to Messiah; all he thought was that it has to be stopped. The thing that Messiah got the chills about the most is that the guys who killed them both were the same skin color as them. *Why do we insist on destroying our own?*

Messiah questioned.

Chapter 12

The fact that we, young black men, get a thrill from killing our

very own is sickening. Also, Messiah felt very sad for the

children that they both left behind. Shine had a daughter and a

son as well as Carlton. The tradition seemed to be put in place

for yet another generation. Carlton's father was killed and

Shine's father was locked up for the majority of his short life.

Now Carlton's son and Shine's son will grow up fatherless.

Messiah would love to help the kids mother's out with raising

them, but he believes they're out of reach they probably have

other young men lined up to be their boyfriends, but they don't

have the best interest in mind for the kids, like Tommy.

Messiah was thinking that more father figures could save the

community, after all Messiah and Rayvon turned out to be ok.

Yes, they both experienced running in the streets and

participating in wrongdoing, but something sparked that

leadership in both of them and Messiah thinks it was their fathers. Big Marcus is truly Messiah's hero and Messiah doesn't mind letting him know. Messiah can't help but think *would I be locked up or dead?* He thinks those are the only two ways out from the lifestyle he was living and quite frankly, the statistics show that's the tragic ending to most young black male stories in urban cities all across the world. Lately, Messiah has been searching for answers. Answers to why all of his brothers can't see the age of 30? Why are his brothers born in the projects anyway? How do they get access to drugs in the projects? Messiah wants to come to peace with this issue before he leaves this Earth. The mission is to grow the mindset of the young black male and, to let these young boys know that your favorite rapper is leading you in the wrong direction. Messiah has no issue against rap, as a matter of fact, he loves rap, mostly conscious rap, but he can get down with the dope beats and other hit songs sometimes too. Messiah seems to love rap with a positive message. He enjoys artists such as Kendrick Lamar, J.Cole, Nas, Jay Z, Meek Mill, and Dee 1. Messiah was listening to Kendrick

Lamar's album *Good Kid Maad City* and he came across a bonus track titled *Black Boy Fly* and he fell in love with the song and the message. This is exactly what Messiah has been trying to figure out for the last couple of years *how can we encourage black boys to fly?*

Chapter 13

With time moving on, it seemed that activities that used to get Messiah excited is now ignorant to him. Going to the mall and spending black dollars on expensive clothes and shoes that are owned by other ethnic groups seems foolish to Messiah today. Turning on the radio to hear these rappers talk about how many women they have, calling our sisters out of their names, and bragging about how many guns they have is foolish to Messiah today. Maybe it's just maturity, but it's not only the young that encourage reckless behavior. Some of the fathers out here are encouraging theirs sons to act out in a negative manner. Messiah is quick to point out a follower from a leader today; he wants to make it his mission to encourage all adolescence to create and follow their own paths. Messiah was once a follower and he knows who is really in the field putting in work and who is pretending. Once before, Big Marcus told Messiah that he was a follower, Messiah had a defensive reaction, and part of the reaction was because he knew that Big Marcus was telling the truth. It's easy to be fed lies like everything will be ok and you're doing fine, but when people tell the truth like Big Marcus did, we get in our feelings but we need to hear this because, that very truth may have changed Messiah's life. Messiah doesn't really get involved with social media today like he used too. Messiah thinks 90 percent of social media is fake. Most people on social media do not live the lives that they put on the internet; instead, they are totally different people in person. Also social media doesn't seem to have any filters when it comes to what we are feeding our children. How easy is it for our children to get on the internet and see a woman naked or a man naked, and these images are on networks such as Facebook, Instagram, and Twitter. Messiah feels that overall in this society that we live in, there is way more negativity than positivity. Why is it way easier to find somebody promoting liquor rather than come across somebody promoting a book to read, especially in the black community? See, in order for our black boys to fly, there has to be a change and not just a change for one or two individuals, we need the whole community to come together to prosper. What does a cool young black man look like in the black community's eyes? Is it having a boatload of women? Being tatted? Having the fanciest clothes and a cool car? The way we are taught today all of these things are qualities that make the freshest and coolest young black males. We need to change that image, how about the black boy who reads two books a month, the black boy who treats every woman in his life like a queen, the black man who gives back to his community with knowledge, and/or the black man who takes care of his seeds. This is Black Boy Fly! In every sense of the meaning, when black boys make our survival as well as our families survival our top priority that's when we will start winning. We have to change our mindset as young black men. We are, for sure, in the midst of a war, whether we know it or not. I really think that black people are the most powerful people on the planet. We seem to master everything that's put in front of us; it can be sports, entertainment, music, or any other industry. Yet, the system is not designed for us to prosper. They might allow a couple of black boys on television or on the football field, but they try to make it as hard as possible for us to prosper on our own, they want to control us and keep us in chains.

Chapter 14

Just sit back and observe how they show us on television the black man is either selling drugs; he's a pimp; a comedian; or he's gay. The music that they sell to us is pushing violence among ourselves, and it's pushing death in our communities. Messiah feels that all of these factors play a role in the murders of not only his friends but young black men all across the globe. We have to save ourselves because nobody else will do it. We need all the strong to help the weak, instead of criticizing their behaviors we need to step back and understand why they are acting in such fashion and try to find a solution. Messiah thought he should put all of these powerful messages into a book; he figured that he had seen enough and the sad part about it is that the violence will continue and, the high rates of incarceration will continue, unless we change. Messiah can't help but think that he is a prime example of a black boy flying. He feels that he is almost free; there is still room for improvement in his own character, but he is definitely far from the place he was in eight or nine years ago as an adolescent. Messiah feels that he has a responsibility to save as many young black males as he can from these struggles. He feels that he can relate to almost everything they are facing, some situations are of course out of his reach but he thinks he can offer them a positive approach to a negative situation. Messiah's biggest goal and dream is for black people, as a community, to be running the game and not just on the field, but in the executive offices or as owners. We should have the power to employ each other, and supply ourselves with everything we need including food, water, clothes, and shelter. If we put as much energy into productive things as we put into Snapchat, and Instagram, we would literally take over everything in a matter of weeks.

Messiah has a vision of blacks starting investing groups,

where everyone can put money in and buy blocks and

neighborhoods those same neighborhoods that we all too

often die in.

Chapter 15

So in the short term what are some ways we can make an

impact in our community today? There are plenty of young

guys standing on the corners of the inner cities today that we

ride pass every day. I challenge you reading this book right

now to try to peacefully approach that young brother and dig

into his brain, try to see the world from his perspective. The

late Biggie Smalls said on the beginning of his song Juicy *"this

album goes out to all the people that lived above the building

that I was hustling in front of that called the police when I was

just tryna make some money to feed my daughter."* My point is

before we judge these young brothers for hanging in the

neighborhoods or hustling let's find out why and if we are so concern then let's try to produce other ways for them to feed their families. What I've found is that the majority of them are acting in the roles as the head of the house hold. These guys are no different from Messiah, Shine, and Raesse they all have the same walks through life, the difference is the support system. Every young king on the corner does not have the same circumstance that Messiah had, so therefore they turn to the streets for love and support. If you look at television shows such as *Beyond Scared Straight,* or any other show that takes you on the inside of the jail house most of the inmates that are in gangs tell the audience they joined the gang for a support system, they didn't receive love at home so they turned to the streets. These guys feel that their gang members are their brothers, as they should because they are, however the gang members are all lost, there are no leaders, at least no responsible leaders. So if you are reading this and you have the heart to approach these young guys to potentially save their lives, do it. A lot of us are quick to judge these young guys but as soon as they get shot by the police such as *Trayvon Martin*, or *Mike Brown* we are quick to rally and scream Black Lives Matter, but we have the power to intervene in these situations before they happened most of the time! To all of you artist that are reading this or anyone who has a following please understand that you do have a responsibility in whatever messages you are putting into the world. If you are a hip-hop artist understand that hip-hop music is the most consumed music genre in the United States most consumed by young black males and females, so whether you accept the title or not you are a role model. Young kids in the inner city's see all the money and flash and that excites them, I challenge you to tell the truth in your music speak on the work you put in to get to your position that you are in today, stop selling these hood dreams to our young people and you are not in that situation today and you may have never lived that life ever. To all my big brothers that are reading this raise the bar for your younger brothers. Stop setting our next generation up for having the freshest clothes and the prettiest girls, challenge our young brothers to read some books that will empower them, there are millions of them available, and you can start with this one. Introduce our young brothers to the stock market, instead of buying the newest iPhone every year buy a stock in Apple, don't just buy these expensive foamposites and Jordan's buy a stock in Nike. Talk to our young brothers about finance before they make any money teach them about saving; explain to them the benefits of saving their money for big purchases such as a home or a car. Lastly explain the idea of ownership to our young brothers, Dr. Boyce Watkins who I have so much respect for says that every black child should know how to start a business by the age of twelve years old, and I agree. The young children growing up in the inner cities are misled about wealth, they are taught that the only ways to get rich are hitting the lottery, landing a record deal, or making it to the NBA or the NFL. We need to be teaching these children the top three ways to obtain wealth are to create a business, invest in the stock market, or to own real estate.

Chapter 16

I'm going to leave you with Messiah's tips for his young kings that are reading this book. To my little brothers reading this watch you're every move, be Sharpe, listen to your parents when they tell you they were once your age, its true! They can save you a lot of time and energy just by listening and paying attention. Also young kings understand that everyone that you are surrounded by is not your friend! A real friend wants the best for you and they will hold you accountable if you're not living up to your best potential. Messiah has seen both sides in case you have not caught on the real friends are the Rayvon's of the world, even if your friend is not on the right track they will push you to stay on the positive path, that's a real friend. Young kings treat these young women as queens; don't imitate these wack rappers who disrespect women. Remember a woman brought you into this world how foolish can you be to call her out of her name or put your hands on her, would you like someone to treat your mother or sister like this? I'm going to leave you with the most important lesson of all, be a leader! Please young kings find yourself and pursue your passion. Whatever your religion is or whoever you believe put you here on earth just know that you are here for a

reason; you have your own personal purpose. Messiah didn't

find his greater self until he took control of his life and stopped

following others.